W9-ABM-951

MARQUEE SERIES

Microsoft® Excel® 2016

Workbook

Nita Rutkosky
Pierce College at Puyallup
Puyallup, Washington

Audrey Roggenkamp
Pierce College at Puyallup
Puyallup, Washington

Ian Rutkosky
Pierce College at Puyallup
Puyallup, Washington

PARADIGM
EDUCATION SOLUTIONS

St. Paul

Senior Vice President	Linda Hein
Editor in Chief	Christine Hurney
Director of Production	Timothy W. Larson
Production Editors	Rachel Kats, Jen Weaverling
Cover and Text Designer	Valerie King
Copy Editor	Sarah Kearin
Senior Design and Production Specialist	Jaana Bykonich
Assistant Developmental Editors	Mamie Clark, Katie Werdick
Testers	Desiree Carvel; Ann E. Mills, Ivy Tech Community College of Indiana, Indianapolis, IN
Instructional Support Writer	Brienna McWade
Indexer	Terry Casey
Vice President Information Technology	Chuck Bratton
Digital Projects Manager	Tom Modl
Vice President Sales and Marketing	Scott Burns
Director of Marketing	Lara Weber McLellan

Care has been taken to verify the accuracy of information presented in this book. However, the authors, editors, and publisher cannot accept responsibility for Web, email, newsgroup, or chat room subject matter or content, or for consequences from application of the information in this book, and make no warranty, expressed or implied, with respect to its content.

Trademarks: Microsoft is a trademark or registered trademark of Microsoft Corporation in the United States and/or other countries. Some of the product names and company names included in this book have been used for identification purposes only and may be trademarks or registered trade names of their respective manufacturers and sellers. The authors, editors, and publisher disclaim any affiliation, association, or connection with, or sponsorship or endorsement by, such owners.

Cover Photo Credits: © whitehoune/Shutterstock.com; © manzrussali/Shutterstock.com.

We have made every effort to trace the ownership of all copyrighted material and to secure permission from copyright holders. In the event of any question arising as to the use of any material, we will be pleased to make the necessary corrections in future printings. Thanks are due to the aforementioned authors, publishers, and agents for permission to use the materials indicated.

ISBN: 978-0-76387-140-6 (print)
ISBN: 978-0-76386-708-9 (digital)

© 2017 by Paradigm Publishing, Inc.
875 Montreal Way
St. Paul, MN 55102
Email: educate@emcp.com
Website: ParadigmCollege.com

All rights reserved. No part of this publication may be adapted, reproduced, stored in a retrieval system, or transmitted in any form or by any means, electronic, mechanical, photocopying, recording, or otherwise, without prior written permission from the publisher.

Printed in the United States of America

24 23 22 21 20 19 18 17   5 6 7 8 9 10 11 12

Microsoft® Excel®

Study Tools

Study tools include a presentation and In Brief step lists. Use these resources to help you further develop and review skills learned in this section.

Knowledge Check

SNAP Check your understanding by identifying application tools used in this section. If you are a SNAP user, launch the Knowledge Check from your Assignments page.

Recheck

SNAP Check your understanding by taking this quiz. If you are a SNAP user, launch the Recheck from your Assignments page.

Skills Exercise

SNAP Additional activities are available to SNAP users. If you are a SNAP user, access these activities from your Assignments page.

Skills Review

Note: If you submit your work in hard copy, check with your instructor before completing these reviews to find out if you need to print two copies of each worksheet with one of the copies showing formulas in cells instead of the calculated results.

Data File

Review 1   Entering Labels, Values, and Formulas

1. Open **WBQtrlyIncome.xlsx** and then save it with the name **1-WBQtrlyIncome**.
2. Type Jul in cell B4.
3. Use the fill handle in cell B4 to enter sequential monthly labels in cells C4 and D4.
4. Type 1300 in cell B11.
5. Use the fill handle in cell B11 to copy the same value to cells C11 and D11.
6. Click in cell B12 and then use the AutoSum button to enter a formula that adds the range B9:B11.
7. Copy the formula in cell B12 to cells C12 and D12.
8. Click in cell B14 and then enter a formula that subtracts the total expenses from gross margin by typing =b7-b12.
9. Copy the formula in cell B14 to cells C14 and D14.
10. Click in cell B15 and then enter a formula that multiplies the net income before taxes by taxes of 22% by typing =b14*.22.
11. Copy the formula in cell B15 to cells C15 and D15.

12. Click in cell B16 and then enter a formula that subtracts the taxes from net income before taxes by typing =b14-b15.
13. Copy the formula in cell B16 to cells C16 and D16.
14. Save **1-WBQtrlyIncome.xlsx**.

Review 2   Improving the Appearance of the Worksheet; Previewing and Printing

1. With **1-WBQtrlyIncome.xlsx** open, merge and center the title in row 1 across columns A through D.
2. Merge and center the text in row 2 across columns A through D.
3. Merge and center the text in row 3 across columns A through D.
4. Change the alignment of the range B4:D4 to right alignment.
5. Apply the Accounting format to the range B5:D16.
6. Display the worksheet in the Print backstage area to preview how the worksheet will look when printed and then print the worksheet. ***Note: If necessary, AutoFit the columns so that all of the data is visible.***
7. Display formulas in the worksheet cells and then print another copy of the worksheet.
8. Turn off the display of formulas in the worksheet.
9. Save and then close **1-WBQtrlyIncome.xlsx**.

Skills Assessment

Note: If you submit your work in hard copy, check with your instructor before completing these assessments to find out if you need to print two copies of each worksheet with one of the copies showing the formulas in cells instead of the calculated results.

Assessment 1   Creating a New Workbook

1. Open Excel and then open a blank workbook.
2. Enter the labels and data in the image in Figure WB-1.1 using the following instructions:
    a. Enter the titles in cells A1 and A2 and then merge and center the ranges A1:G1 and A2:G2.
    b. Enter the labels in column A and then AutoFit column A by double-clicking the boundary between the column A and column B headings.
    c. Enter the remaining labels and data using the fill handle to enter repetitive or series data. (Type the percentage sign after the number *85* in column F.)
3. Enter the following formulas in the worksheet:
    a. Enter a SUM function in cell E4 that totals the values in the range B4:D4 and then use the fill handle to copy the formula into cell E9.
    b. Enter a SUM function in cell B10 that totals the values in the range B4:B9 and then use the fill handle to copy the formula into cell E10.
    c. Enter a formula in G4 that multiplies the subtotal in cell E4 by the exchange rate in cell F4 and then copy the formula into cell G10.
4. Apply the Accounting format to the appropriate cells.

5. Apply alignment and font formatting options you learned in this section as needed to improve the appearance of the worksheet.
6. AutoFit columns that do not display the full contents of the cells.
7. Save the workbook with the name **1-MPExpenses**.
8. Preview the worksheet, change to landscape orientation, and then print the worksheet.
9. Close **1-MPExpenses.xlsx**.

Figure WB-1.1 Assessment 1

	A	B	C	D	E	F	G
1				Marquee Productions			
2				Filming Expenses July - September 2018			
3		Jul	Aug	Sep	Subtotal	Exchange Rate	Total
4	Actors/Actresses	22000	24500	20150		85%	
5	AV Equipment	16050	16050	16050		85%	
6	Costume Rental	8900	8900	8900		85%	
7	Catering	3950	4850	3700		85%	
8	Location Fees	12050	12050	12050		85%	
9	Transportation	5500	5900	5700		85%	
10	Total					85%	
11							

Assessment 2   Entering Formulas and Editing Data

1. Open **FCTSales.xlsx** and then save it with the name **1-FCTSales**.
2. Enter a SUM function in cell F4 that sums the four quarter sales figures for Jonas Arund.
3. Use the fill handle to copy the formula in cell F4 down into cell F9.
4. Enter a formula in cell G4 that multiplies the total sales (cell F4) by a 9% commission for Jonas Arund. ***Hint: Type the commission percent as .09.***
5. Use the fill handle to copy the formula in cell G4 down into cell G9.
6. Make cell A8 active and then edit the last name so it does not include the *s* (it should read *Frank*).
7. Make cell C8 active and then replace the cell contents with the value *34541*.
8. Make cell E7 active and then replace the cell contents with the value *29848*.
9. Undo the last action.
10. Apply alignment and formatting options you learned in this section as needed to improve the appearance of the worksheet.
11. Save, print, and then close **1-FCTSales.xlsx**.

Assessment 3   Creating a New Workbook

1. Open Excel and then create a new workbook that tracks how many First Choice Travel bookings are made for various cities, the average sale price for each city, and a total sales estimate for each city using the following instructions:
   a. Enter the company name, *First Choice Travel*, in the first row and a title for the worksheet in the second row.
   b. Enter the labels and values in Table WB-1.1, starting with the label City in cell A3.
   c. Enter the label Total Sales Estimate in cell D3 with a manual line break inserted between the words Sales and Estimate.
2. Enter a formula in cell D4 that multiplies the bookings by the average sale price.

Table WB-1.1 Assessment 3

City	Bookings	Average Sale Price
New York	89	3890
Tucson	23	2785
Los Angeles	104	3740
Denver	36	2610
Orlando	62	3170
Des Moines	9	1925
Wichita	8	2100
Boston	41	3170
Philadelphia	21	1970
Dallas	56	2435
Milwaukee	13	2615
Atlanta	40	2690
Vancouver	37	3420
Calgary	28	3295
Toronto	23	2855
Montreal	38	2660

3. Use the fill handle to copy the formula through cell D19.
4. Apply alignment and formatting options you learned in this section as needed to improve the appearance of the worksheet.
5. Use the Tell Me feature to change the font color for the company name in cell A1 to standard blue.
6. Save the workbook with the name **1-FCTCities**.
7. Turn on the display of formulas.
8. Print and then close **1-FCTCities.xlsx**.

Worldwide Enterprises

Data File

Assessment 4   Finding Information on Number Formatting

1. In Activity 1.9, you learned how to apply the Accounting format. Other number formats are available for different purposes. Use the Tell Me feature or Excel Help feature to find out how to apply the Comma and Percentage number formats to cells and decrease the amount of digits that display after the decimal point.
2. Open **WEBudget.xlsx** and then save it with the name **1-WEBudget**.
3. Apply the Comma format (using the Comma Style button) to the range B5:C15 and remove any digits that display after the decimal point.
4. Apply the Percentage format (using the Percent Style button) to the range D4:D17.
5. Print the worksheet.
6. Save and then close **1-WEBudget.xlsx**.

INDIVIDUAL CHALLENGE

Assessment 5   Creating a School Budget

1. Create a worksheet to calculate the estimated total cost of completing your diploma or certificate. You determine the items that need to be included in the worksheet, such as tuition, fees, textbooks, supplies, accommodation costs, transportation, telephone, food, and entertainment. If necessary, use the Internet to find reasonable cost estimates if you want to include an item such as cell phone charges and want to research competitive rates for your area. Arrange the labels and values by quarter,

semester, or academic year according to your preference. Make sure to include a total that shows the total cost of your education.

2. Save the workbook with the name **1-SchoolBudget**.
3. Apply alignment and formatting options you learned in this section as needed to improve the appearance of the worksheet.
4. If necessary, change to landscape orientation and then print the worksheet.
5. Save and then close **1-SchoolBudget.xlsx**.

Marquee Challenge

Challenge 1 Preparing an International Student Registration Report

1. You work at Niagara Peninsula College in the Registrar's Office. The Registrar has asked you to create the annual report for international student registrations. Create the worksheet shown in Figure WB-1.2.
2. Calculate the tuition fees in column I by multiplying the credit hours times the fee per hour and then use the SUM function to calculate the total international student fees.
3. Apply format options as shown and apply the Accounting format to the amounts in columns H and I.
4. Add the current date and your name in rows 4 and 18, respectively.
5. Change to landscape orientation.
6. Save the workbook with the name **1-NPCIntlRegRpt**.
7. Print and then close **1-NPCIntlRegRpt.xlsx**.

Figure WB-1.2 Challenge 1

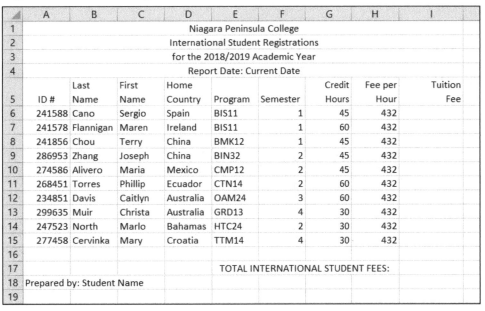

	A	B	C	D	E	F	G	H	I
1				Niagara Peninsula College					
2				International Student Registrations					
3				for the 2018/2019 Academic Year					
4				Report Date: Current Date					
5	ID #	Last Name	First Name	Home Country	Program	Semester	Credit Hours	Fee per Hour	Tuition Fee
6	241588	Cano	Sergio	Spain	BIS11	1	45	432	
7	241578	Flannigan	Maren	Ireland	BIS11	1	60	432	
8	241856	Chou	Terry	China	BMK12	1	45	432	
9	286953	Zhang	Joseph	China	BIN32	2	45	432	
10	274586	Alivero	Maria	Mexico	CMP12	2	45	432	
11	268451	Torres	Phillip	Ecuador	CTN14	2	60	432	
12	234851	Davis	Caitlyn	Australia	OAM24	3	60	432	
13	299635	Muir	Christa	Australia	GRD13	4	30	432	
14	247523	North	Marlo	Bahamas	HTC24	2	30	432	
15	277458	Cervinka	Mary	Croatia	TTM14	4	30	432	
16									
17					TOTAL INTERNATIONAL STUDENT FEES:				
18	Prepared by: Student Name								
19									

Challenge 2 Preparing a Theatre Arts Target Enrollment Report

1. You work with Cal Rubine, chair of the Theatre Arts Division at Niagara Peninsula College. Cal needs the target student enrollment report to assist with the revenue projections for the upcoming budget. Cal has asked you to create the worksheet shown in Figure WB-1.3.

Figure WB-1.3 Challenge 2

	A	B	C	D	E	F
1	Niagara Peninsula College					
2	Theatre Arts Division					
3	Target Student Enrollments					
4	for the 2018/2019 Academic Year					
5						
6	Academic chair: Cal Rubine					
7						
8	Program Name	Program Code	Semester Offering	Target Percent	Actual Enrollment 2017/2018	Target Enrollment
9	Theatre Arts: Acting	TAA12	1 2 3 4		210	
10	Theatre Arts: Stage Management	TAM23	1 2		55	
11	Theatre Arts: Lighting & Effects	TAL42	1 2		67	
12	Theatre Arts: Production	TAP32	1 2 3 4		221	
13	Theatre Arts: Sound	TAS14	1 2		38	
14	Theatre Arts: Businsess Management	TAB25	1 2 3 4		64	
15						
16			ESTIMATED ENROLLMENTS FOR 2018/2019:			
17						
18	Report date: Current Date					
19	Prepared by: Student Name					
20						

2. Cal uses the actual enrollments from the prior year (2017/2018) to calculate the target for the next year. In some programs, Cal expects that enrollment will be higher than the previous year due to new registrants, transfers from other programs, and students returning to pick up missed credits. In other programs, Cal expects that enrollment will decline from the previous year due to students dropping the program, transferring to other colleges, and failing to meet the minimum GPA for progression. Cal has provided the percentages in Table WB-1.2 for you to use to create the formulas in the *Target Percent* column. Insert the target percent in the worksheet and then enter a formula in column F to determine the target enrollment.
3. Use the SUM function in cell F16 to calculate the total estimated enrollments.
4. Autofit columns A, E, and F.
5. Apply alignment options as shown and add the current date and your name in rows 18 and 19, respectively.
6. If necessary, format the values in the *Target Percent* column to zero digits past the decimal point and the values in the *Target Enrollment* column to two digits past the decimal point.
7. Change to landscape orientation.
8. Save the workbook with the name **1-NPCTargetEnrolRpt**.
9. Print and then close **1-NPCTargetEnrolRpt.xlsx**.

Table WB-1.2 Challenge 2

Program Name	Target Percent
Theatre Arts: Acting	95%
Theatre Arts: Stage Management	106%
Theatre Arts: Lighting & Effects	112%
Theatre Arts: Production	85%
Theatre Arts: Sound	103%
Theatre Arts: Business Management	75%

Study Tools

SNAP Study tools include a presentation and In Brief step lists. Use these resources to help you further develop and review skills learned in this section.

Knowledge Check

SNAP Check your understanding by identifying application tools used in this section. If you are a SNAP user, launch the Knowledge Check from your Assignments page.

Recheck

SNAP Check your understanding by taking this quiz. If you are a SNAP user, launch the Recheck from your Assignments page.

Skills Exercise

SNAP Additional activities are available to SNAP users. If you are a SNAP user, access these activities from your Assignments page.

Skills Review

Review 1   Editing, Moving, Copying, and Clearing Cells; Performing a Spell Check; Inserting and Deleting Rows

Data File

1. Open **WBInvToNPC.xlsx** and save it with the name **2-WBInvToNPC**.
2. Change the amount in cell D20 from *13.73* to *15.23*.
3. Clear the contents of cell A8.
4. Change the label in cell A21 from *Soup* to *French Onion Soup*.
5. Type new data in the cells indicated.

    E14   PO No.   F14   TA-11-643
6. Delete rows 7, 8, and 9.
7. Complete a spelling check of the worksheet. (All names are spelled correctly.)
8. Move the range E7:F7 to E10:F10.
9. Copy cell A24 to cell A30.
10. Delete the rows that contain the labels *Milk* and *Donuts*.
11. Insert a new row between *Prime Rib* and *Mixed Vegetables* and then type Seafood Pasta in column A of the new row.
12. Save **2-WBInvToNPC.xlsx**.

Review 2   Adjusting Column Widths; Replacing Data; Moving Cells

1. With **2-WBInvToNPC.xlsx** open, adjust the width of column A to 17.00 characters.
2. Change the width of column C to the length of the longest entry (AutoFit).
3. Change the width of column D to 17.00 characters and column E to 7.00 characters.
4. Use the Replace feature to replace the value *32* with *36* for all occurrences.
5. Create a SUM formula in cell F33 to total cells F17 through F31.
6. Apply numeric formats as follows:
   a. Apply the Accounting format to cells F17 and F33.
   b. Apply the Comma format (using the Comma Style button) to cells F28 and F31.
7. Indent one time the ranges A18:A27 and A29:A30.
8. Select the range D1:D3 and then change the font to 10-point Cambria bold.
9. Move the range D1:D3 to F1:F3 and then align the text at the right edge of the cells.
10. Save **2-WBInvToNPC.xlsx**.

Review 3   Applying Formatting Features; Inserting an Image

Data File

1. With **2-WBInvToNPC.xlsx** open, merge and center and then apply the Input cell style (in the *Data and Model* section) to the range A17:B17 and A28:B28.
2. Merge and center cell A5 across columns A through F and then apply the Title cell style (in the *Titles and Headings* section) to cell A5.
3. Center the values in columns C and D and the labels in the range C16:F16.
4. Add a top and bottom border to the range A16:F16 and apply bold formatting.
5. Add a top and double bottom border to cell F33 and apply bold formatting.
6. Add an outside border to the range A1:F36.
7. Add the fill color Green, Accent 6, Lighter 80% (last column, second row in *Theme Colors* section) to cell A5.
8. Add the fill color Green, Accent 6, Lighter 60% (last column, third row in the *Theme Colors* section) to the range A16:F16.
9. Apply the Integral theme to the worksheet.
10. Apply the Green Yellow theme colors.
11. Make cell A1 the active cell and then insert the image **TWBLogo.jpg**.
12. Change the height of the image to 0.75 inch.
13. Save, print, and then close **2-WBInvToNPC.xlsx**.

Skills Assessment

Note: If you submit your work in hard copy, check with your instructor before completing these Assessments to find out if you need to print two copies of each worksheet, with one of the copies showing the cell formulas instead of the calculated results.

Assessment 1   Editing Cells; Inserting Columns; Copying Formulas; Inserting Images; Applying Formatting Features

Data Files

1. Open **PTMarqCost.xlsx** and save it with the name **2-PTMarqCost**.
2. Complete the worksheet using the following information:
   a. Design costs for all costumes should display as *122.50* instead of *22*.

b. Insert a new column between *Fabric* and *Total Cost* and type the column heading Notions in cell I3. Type the values in the range I4:I10 as follows:

Henry II	101.50	John	47.85
Queen Eleanor	88.23	Geoffrey	47.85
Alias	58.40	Philip	47.85
Richard	47.85		

c. The formula to calculate total cost for each costume is incorrect. Enter the correct formula for the first costume (cell J4) and then copy the formula to the range J5:J10. *Hint: The current formula does not include the fabric and notions costs. Add the correct cells to the end of the formula.*

d. Create a formula in cell K4 to calculate the costume fee that will multiply the total cost in cell J4 by 1.5 and then copy the formula to the range K5:K10.

e. Create a formula in cell L4 to calculate the profit as costume fee minus total cost and then copy the formula to the range L5:L10.

f. Format the numeric cells in an appropriate style.

g. Change the alignment of any headings that could be improved in appearance.

h. Merge and center the titles in cells A1 and A2 over columns A to L.

i. Adjust the height of row 1 to 54.00 points and row 2 to 30.00 points.

j. Insert the image **PTLogo.jpg** and then resize it to fit in the top row at the top left of the worksheet.

k. Apply font, border, and color changes to enhance the appearance of the worksheet. Adjust column widths as needed.

l. Change to landscape orientation.

3. Save, print, and then close **2-PTMarqCost.xlsx**.

Assessment 2 Completing and Formatting a Worksheet

Data Files

1. Open **PTMarqCostInv.xlsx** and save it with the name **2-PTMarqCostInv**.

2. Complete the invoice using the following information:

a. Type the current date in cell G6.

b. Refer to your electronic copy or printout of the costumes in Assessment 1. Type the values from the *Fee* column (the range K4:K10) into the appropriate cells in the range F15:F21.

c. Create a formula to total the costume fees in cell F22. *Hint: Make sure the total agrees with the total costume fee on your printout from Assessment 1.*

d. The transportation and storage container fee for each of the seven costumes is $75.00. Enter the appropriate formula in cell F24 that will calculate the fee for seven containers.

e. Enter in cell F25 the delivery fee for all seven costumes: $250.00.

f. Enter in cell F26 a formula that will add the total for the costume fees with the additional charges.

g. Enter in cell F27 a formula that will calculate 13% Canadian Harmonized sales tax on the total in cell F26.

h. Enter in cell F28 a formula to calculate the total invoice as the sum of cells F26 and F27.

3. Insert **PTLogo.jpg** in cell A1 and then resize it to fit in the three rows at the top left of the worksheet.

4. Improve the appearance of the worksheet by adjusting column widths, deleting blank rows, moving cells, and/or applying formatting features that you learned in this section.
5. Save, print, and then close **2-PTMarqCostInv.xlsx**.

Assessment 3   Performing a Spelling Check; Adjusting Column Width; Using Find and Replace; Inserting an Image; Applying Formatting Features

Data File

1. Open **WEMPRev.xlsx** and save it with the name **2-WEMPRev**.
2. Make the following corrections:
   a. Perform a spelling check.
   b. Adjust column widths so all data is completely visible.
   c. Change all of the venues named *Cinema House* to *Cinema Magic*.
   d. In cell A3, type Date: and then enter today's date in cell B3.
   e. Search for an image of a monarch butterfly and then insert the image at the top right of the worksheet.
   f. Improve the appearance of the worksheet by applying formatting features you learned in this section.
3. Save, print, and then close **2-WEMPRev.xlsx**.

Assessment 4   Finding Scaling Options

1. Open **WBInventory.xlsx** and then save it with the name **2-WBInventory**.
2. Use the Help feature to find out how to scale a worksheet so it fits on one page when printed.
3. Click the File tab and then click the *Print* option to display the Print backstage area.
4. Scale the worksheet so that it fits on one page at the Print backstage area.
5. Print, save, and then close **2-WBInventory.xlsx**.

INDIVIDUAL CHALLENGE

Assessment 5   Locating Information on Theatre Arts Programs

1. You are considering enrolling in a drama/theatre arts program at a college or university. Search the Internet for available programs in postsecondary schools in the United States and Canada. Choose three schools that interest you the most and find out as much as you can about the costs of attending these schools. Try to find information on costs beyond tuition and books, such as transportation and room and board.
2. Create a workbook that compares the costs for each of the three schools. For example, create the cost categories in column A and include three columns next to each cost category where you will enter the costs you found for each school. Total the costs for each of the schools.
3. Apply formatting features you learned in this section to the worksheet.
4. Save the workbook with the name **2-TheatreArts**.
5. Print and then close **2-TheatreArts.xlsx**.

Marquee Challenge

Challenge 1   Creating a Direct Wages Budget Report for a Film Shoot

1. You work with Chris Greenbaum, production manager at Marquee Productions. Chris has asked you to create the direct wages budget for the company's remote location film shoot. Create the worksheet shown in Figure WB-2.1. *Note: The logo is a file named MPLogo.jpg*.
2. Link the values in the *Estimated Daily Rates* table (columns I and J) to the *Daily Rate* column (column F) in the budget section.
3. Calculate the extended cost by summing the number of days for site prep, shoot, and cleanup and then multiplying by the daily rate.
4. Calculate the total in cell G16.
5. Apply formatting options as shown and then format the values in column G to an appropriate number format. Use your best judgment to determine the font, font size, column widths, borders, and fill colors.
6. Although not visible in the figure, a border should also be applied along the top (columns A–G) and left edges (rows 1–16) of the budget cells so that, when printed, the entire budget has a perimeter border.
7. Print the worksheet in landscape orientation and then save it with the name **2-MPLocBudg**.
8. Close **2-MPLocBudg.xlsx**.

Challenge 2   Creating a Room Timetable

1. You are an assistant to the person who schedules classroom space in the Theatre Arts Division at Niagara Peninsula College. You have been given the room schedule for the auditorium for next semester. The division posts a printed copy of the timetable outside the auditorium door so that students know when the room is available to work on projects and rehearse for upcoming plays. You want to use Excel to create and format the timetable so that the printed copy is easy to read and has a more professional appearance.
2. Refer to the data in Figure WB-2.2 and then create the timetable in a new workbook. Apply formatting features you learned in this section to create a colorful, easy-to-read room timetable.
3. Save the workbook with the name **2-NPCRoomSch**.
4. Print and then close **2-NPCRoomSch.xlsx**.

Figure WB-2.1 Challenge 1

	A	B	C	D	E	F	G	H	I	J
1										
2			MARQUEE PRODUCTIONS							
3										
4			Remove Location Film Shoot							
			July 11 to Agust 31, 2018							
5			Direct Wages Budget							
6			Site Prep	Shoot	Cleanup	Daily	Extended		Estimated Daily Rates	
7	Personnel		Days	Days	Days	Rate	Cost		Subject to Change	
8	Crew		9	32	2				Crew	1,275
9	Cast		0	32	0				Cast	13,775
10	Actor Assistants		0	32	0				Actor Assistants	3,250
11	Extras		0	19	0				Extras	2,800
12	Cleaners		9	32	5				Cleaners	875
13	Security		7	32	5				Security	3,750
14	Administration		9	32	5				Administration	1,275
15										
16				Total Direct Wages Budget						
17										

Figure WB-2.2 Challenge 2

Niagara Peninsula College					
Room:	T1101		Period Covered: January 1 to April 30		
Time	Monday	Tuesday	Wednesday	Thursday	Friday
8:00 AM	SM100-01	AC215-03		MG210-01	SM240-03
9:00 AM	Prasad	McLean	LE100-03	Spelberger	Prasad
10:00 AM	LE253-03	(lab)	Das	SM355-02	SD350-04
11:00 AM	Das			Prasad	Attea
12:00 PM	SD451-01	PD250-02	Common	PD320-03	
1:00 PM	Attea	Kemper	Period	Kemper	LE310-02
2:00 PM	PD340-02	MG410-03	AC478-01	AC480-01	Das
3:00 PM	Kemper	Spelberger	Simmons	Simmons	MG210-01
4:00 PM	MG150-02	SM165-01	AC140-01	(lab)	Spelberger
5:00 PM	Spelberger	Prasad	Chou		

Use of this facility is restricted to staff and registered students only of Niagara Peninsula College. Failure to abide by this policy is considered a serious violation of the college's code of conduct.

Note 1:	Monday through Thursday evenings, room is booked for Continuing Education department.
Note 2:	Room is booked 8:00 AM to 5:00 PM the second Saturday of each month for the local community theatre group.

Study Tools

Study tools include a presentation and In Brief step lists. Use these resources to help you further develop and review skills learned in this section.

Knowledge Check

 SNAP Check your understanding by identifying application tools used in this section. If you are a SNAP user, launch the Knowledge Check from your Assignments page.

Recheck

 SNAP Check your understanding by taking this quiz. If you are a SNAP user, launch the Recheck from your Assignments page.

Skills Exercise

 SNAP Additional activities are available to SNAP users. If you are a SNAP user, access these activities from your Assignments page.

Skills Review

Review 1 Inserting Statistical, Date, and IF Functions; Creating Range Names; Changing Page Layout Options

Data File

1. Open **WBQtrRev.xlsx** and then save it with the name **3-WBQtrRev**.
2. Select the range B10:E10 and name it *TotalQtr*.
3. Make cell B12 active and then insert a formula that finds the average of the TotalQtr range.
4. Make cell B13 active and then insert a formula that finds the maximum total quarterly revenue in the TotalQtr range.
5. Make cell B14 active and then insert a formula that finds the minimum total quarterly revenue in the TotalQtr range.
6. Make cell B16 active and then name the cell *MinTarget*.
7. Make cell B17 active and then calculate how much under the minimum target the quarter's total revenue is if the minimum target was not met by typing the IF formula =if(b10<mintarget,b10-mintarget,0).
8. Copy the IF formula in cell B17 to the range C17:E17.
9. Make cell B19 active and then format the date in the cell to display as *#/##/##*.

10. Make cell B20 active and then insert a formula that adds 350 days to the date in cell B19.
11. Change to landscape orientation.
12. Change the top margin to 1.5 inches and center the worksheet horizontally.
13. Display the worksheet in Page Layout view and then create a header that prints your first and last names at the left margin and the current date at the right margin.
14. Create a footer that prints the file name at the bottom center of the page.
15. Save and then print **3-WBQtrRev.xlsx**.

Review 2   Creating Charts; Drawing Shapes

1. With **3-WBQtrRev.xlsx** open, select the range A3:E8 and then create a column chart by completing the following steps:
   a. Click the *Clustered Column* option in the *2-D Column* section.
   b. Move the chart to a new sheet and label the sheet *ColumnChart*.
   c. Apply the Layout 5 quick layout.
   d. Apply the Style 6 chart style.
   e. Change the chart title to *Quarterly Revenue Budget Forecast*.
   f. Select and then delete the Axis Title box that displays rotated at the left side of the chart.
2. Print the ColumnChart sheet.
3. Make Sheet1 the active sheet, select the ranges A3:A8 and F3:F8, and then create a pie chart by completing the following steps:
   a. Click the *Pie* option in the *2-D Pie* section.
   b. Move the chart to a new sheet and label the sheet *PieChart*.
   c. Apply the Layout 6 quick layout.
   d. Apply the Style 3 chart style.
   e. Change the chart title to *Total Revenue Budget Forecast*.
   f. Select the legend and then change the font size to 11 points.
4. With PieChart the active sheet, draw an Up Arrow Callout shape (last shape in second row in the *Block Arrows* group) in the pie chart by completing the following steps:
   a. Click the *Up Arrow Callout* shape and then click directly below the *55%* in the Dining room pie slice.
   b. Change the height of the shape to 1.4 inches and the width to 1.6 inches.
   c. Type This is a 10% increase over last year! inside the shape.
   d. Position the arrow below *55%* with the tip of the arrow touching the middle of the bottom border of the *55%*.
   e. With the shape selected, click the Home tab, click the Bold button in the Font group, and then click the Center button and the Middle Align button in the Alignment group.
5. Print the PieChart sheet.
6. Save and then close **3-WBQtrRev.xlsx**.

Skills Assessment

Note: If you submit your work in hard copy, check with your instructor before completing these Assessments to find out if you need to print two copies of each worksheet with one of the copies showing the cell formulas instead of the calculated results.

Assessment 1 Creating Statistical and IF Functions; Using Absolute References

1. Open **FCTSalesComm.xlsx** and then save it with the name **3-FCTSalesComm**.
2. Make cell D4 active and then write an IF statement using the information in the Commission table in the range F2:G4. Write the IF statement so that if the number of cruises booked is greater than 2, then Excel will multiply the total value of travel bookings by the commission percentage in cell G4, and if the condition is not met, Excel will insert a zero. Note: When a zero has the Accounting format applied, it displays as a hyphen instead of a 0. You will be copying the formula, so make sure cell G4 in the formula is an absolute reference.
3. Copy the IF function in cell D4 into cell D16.
4. Format the values in column D to match the formatting of the numbers in column B.
5. Type the label Average commission in cell B20 and create a function in cell D20 to calculate the average commission paid.
6. Type the label Maximum commission in cell B21 and create a function in cell D21 to show the highest commission paid.
7. Scale the worksheet to fit on one page.
8. Change the top margin to 1.25 inches and the left margin to 1.5 inches.
9. Save, print, and then close **3-FCTSalesComm.xlsx**.

Assessment 2 Applying the PMT Function

1. Open **WELoan.xlsx** and then save it with the name **3-WELoan**.
2. Calculate the monthly payments on the loan in cells B7 and D7.
3. Calculate the total payments required for each loan in cells B11 and D11.
4. Save, print, and then close **3-WELoan.xlsx**.

Assessment 3 Creating Charts; Drawing Shapes

1. Open **NPCGrades.xlsx** and then save it with the name **3-NPCGrades**.
2. Create a line chart in a new sheet labeled *LineChart* that displays the number of A+ through F grades earned for all five courses. Include an appropriate chart title. You determine the line chart style, layout, and any other chart elements and formats that will make the chart easy to interpret.
3. Create a 3-D pie chart that displays the total of each grade as a percentage of 100. *Hint: Select the ranges B3:G3 and B9:G9 to create the chart.* Include an appropriate chart title and display percents around the outside of the pie slices as well as the category names. Position the pie chart below the grades worksheet, starting in row 11.

4. In the white space at the top left of the chart, draw a right-pointing block arrow pointing to the percent value above the pie slice for the F grade. Inside the block arrow type the text Lowest failure rate since 2014! If necessary, format the text to a smaller font to fit within the available space.

5. Print the worksheet centered horizontally and then print the line chart.

6. Save and then close **3-NPCGrades.xlsx**.

Assessment 4   Creating Charts; Changing Page Layout; Inserting a Footer

1. Open **FCTEurope.xlsx** and then save it with the name **3-FCTEurope**.

2. Create a 3-D Clustered Bar bar chart in a new sheet labeled *14NightsChart* that graphs the standard and deluxe rates for all of the destinations for 14 nights. Add an appropriate title to the chart and make any other formatting choices you think would enhance the chart.

3. Print the 14NightsChart sheet.

4. Create a 3-D Clustered Bar bar chart in a new sheet labeled *21NightsChart* that graphs the standard and deluxe rates for all of the destinations for 21 nights. Add an appropriate title to the chart and make any other formatting choices you think would enhance the chart.

5. Print the 21NightsChart sheet.

6. Make Sheet1 the active sheet, change to landscape orientation, change the top margin to 1.5 inches, and center the worksheet horizontally.

7. Create a custom footer that prints your name at the left margin and the file name at the right margin.

8. Print Sheet1.

9. Save and then close **3-FCTEurope.xlsx**.

Assessment 5   Finding Information on Chart Axis Options

1. Use the Help feature to find information on changing the vertical axis scale options in a chart. Use *change axis labels* as the search text.

2. Open **3-FCTEurope.xlsx**.

3. Make the 14NightsChart sheet active.

4. Using the information you learned in Help, change the value axis options so that the minimum bounds value is fixed at 1,000 and the major unit is fixed at 500. This means the value axis will start at $1,000 instead of zero and gridlines will show at every $500 interval. ***Hint: Make these changes in the Format Axis task pane with the Axis Options icon selected.***

5. Print the 14NightsChart sheet.

6. Save and then close **3-FCTEurope.xlsx**.

Assessment 6   Social Networking Survey

1. You want to know which social networking tool and which social activity is the most popular among your friends, family, and classmates. Ask 10 to 20 friends, family, or classmates the following two questions and collect the responses in an Excel worksheet.
   a. Which of the following social networking sites do you use?

   Facebook   Instagram
   Pinterest   Twitter

   b. Which social networking activities do you do at these sites?

   Share photos   Share family updates
   Promote a blog   Share media
   Meet people

2. Create a chart in a new sheet labeled *SocialNetSites* that displays the total users for each of the social networking sites in the first survey question. You determine the most appropriate chart type to display the survey results. Add an appropriate chart title and any other chart formatting options to enhance the chart's appearance.

3. Print the SocialNetSites sheet.

4. Create a chart in a new sheet labeled *SocialNetAct* that displays the total participants for each type of social networking activity in the second survey question. You determine the appropriate chart type to display the survey results. Add an appropriate chart title and any other chart formatting options to enhance the chart's appearance.

5. Print the SocialNetAct sheet.

6. Save the workbook and name it **3-SocialNetSurvey**.

7. Print the worksheet with the source data for the two charts and then close **3-SocialNetSurvey.xlsx**.

Marquee Challenge

Challenge 1   Creating Charts on Movie Attendance Statistics

1. You are working with Shannon Grey, president of Marquee Productions, on presentation materials for an upcoming staff development workshop on producing and marketing movies. As part of Shannon's research for the workshop, she compiled a workbook with statistics related to movie attendance by age group and by household income. Shannon has asked you to create two charts for the workshop based on this source data. To begin, open **MPMovieStats.xlsx** and then save it with the name **3-MPMovieStats**.

2. Using data in the workbook, create the bar chart in Figure WB-3.1 with the following specifications:
   a. Create a 3-D Clustered Bar chart.
   b. Move the chart to a new sheet and name the sheet *AgeChart*.
   c. Apply the Style 6 chart style.
   d. Change the font for the title to 20-point Cambria bold.
   e. Add the primary horizontal axis to the chart using the Chart Elements button. *Hint: Expand the **Axes** option and then insert a check mark in the **Primary Horizontal** check box.*

f. Change the font for the axes (information at the left and bottom) to 12-point Cambria bold and change the font color to White, Background 1.

g. Insert the shape with the Down Arrow Callout shape in the *Block Arrows* section.

h. Make any other formatting changes so your chart looks like the chart in Figure WB-3.1.

3. Using data in the workbook, create the Doughnut chart in Figure WB-3.2 with the following specifications:

a. Create a Doughnut chart. (Use the Insert Pie or Doughnut Chart button in the Charts group on the Insert tab to find the doughnut chart.)

b. Move the chart to a new sheet and name the sheet *IncomeChart*.

c. Apply the Style 3 chart style.

d. Apply the Layout 5 chart layout.

e. Change the font for the title to 20-point Cambria bold.

f. Insert the 8-Point Star shape (fifth column, first row in the *Stars and Banners* section).

g. Make any other formatting changes so your chart looks like the chart in Figure WB-3.2.

4. Save the revised workbook.

5. Print each chart and then close **3-MPMovieStats.xlsx**.

Figure WB-3.1 Challenge 1 Bar Chart

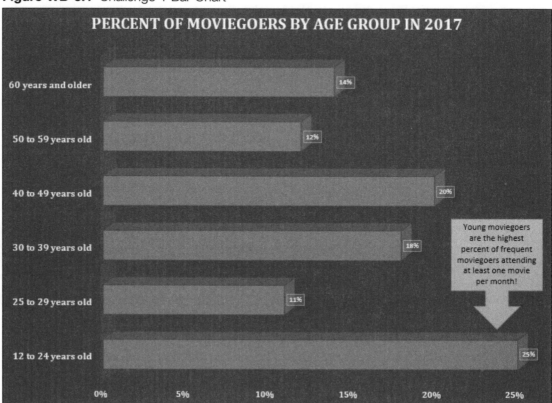

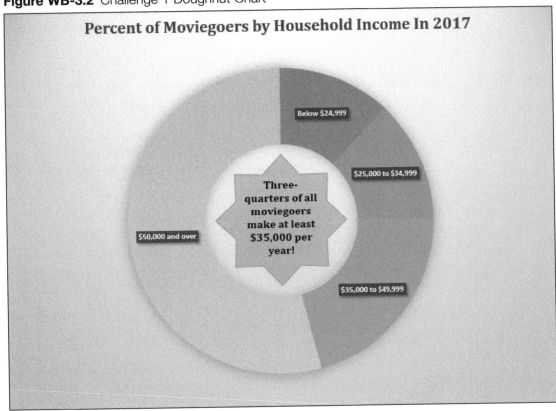

Percent of Moviegoers by Household Income In 2017

Below $24,999

$25,000 to $34,999

Three-quarters of all moviegoers make at least $35,000 per year!

$50,000 and over

$35,000 to $49,999

Niagara Peninsula College

Data Files

Challenge 2   Preparing an International Student Report

1. You work in the Registrar's Office at Niagara Peninsula College. Terri VanDaele, the registrar, has sent you a workbook with the top 10 countries of origin for international students registered for the 2018 academic year. Terri would like you to format the workbook to improve the appearance and create a chart next to the data for inclusion with the annual report to the board. To begin, open **NPCTop10Int.xlsx** and then save it with the name **3-NPCTop10Int**.

2. Using the data in the workbook, create the chart shown in Figure WB-3.3. Create a 2-D clustered column chart, apply the Style 4 chart style, and delete the title. Size and move the chart so it is positioned as shown in the figure.

3. Insert and position the Niagara Peninsula College logo as shown in the figure using the **NPCLogo.jpg** file.

4. Insert the image **GlobeHands.jpg** and then size and move the image so it appears as shown in the figure.

5. Make sure the workbook fits on one page. If it does not, change to landscape orientation.

6. Save, print, and then close **3-NPCTop10Int.xlsx**.

Figure WB-3.3 Challenge 2

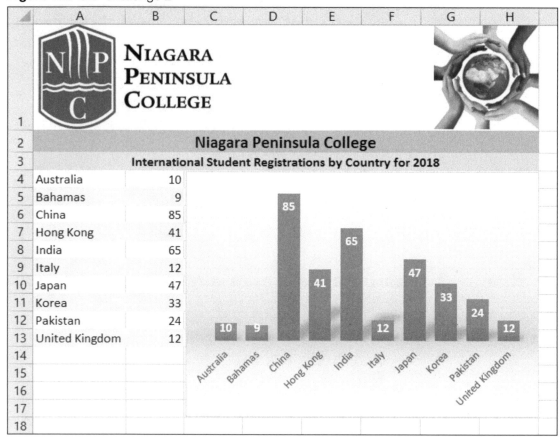

Excel Section 4

Working with Multiple Worksheets, Tables, and Other File Formats

> **Study Tools**

Study tools include a presentation and In Brief step lists. Use these resources to help you further develop and review skills learned in this section.

> **Knowledge Check**

 Check your understanding by identifying application tools used in this section. If you are a SNAP user, launch the Knowledge Check from your Assignments page.

> **Recheck**

 Check your understanding by taking this quiz. If you are a SNAP user, launch the Recheck from your Assignments page.

Skills Exercise

 Additional activities are available to SNAP users. If you are a SNAP user, access these activities from your Assignments page.

Skills Review

Note: If you submit your work in hard copy, check with your instructor before completing these reviews to find out if you need to print two copies of each worksheet with one of the copies showing formulas in cells instead of the calculated results.

> **Data File**

Review 1   **Managing and Formatting Worksheets; Using 3-D References; Printing Multiple Worksheets**

1. Open **WBPayroll.xlsx** and then save it with the name **4-WBPayroll**.
2. Delete the Week4 worksheet.
3. Copy the Week3 worksheet and position the new worksheet after Week3.
4. Rename the Week3 (2) worksheet as Week4.
5. Make the Week4 worksheet active and then edit the following cells:
    Change cell C3 from *11/23/2018* to *11/30/18*.
    Change cell C11 from *0* to *8*.
    Change cell G11 from *9* to *0*.
    Change cell I14 from *6* to *9*.
6. Apply the standard dark blue tab color to the Week1 through Week4 worksheet tabs and the standard dark red tab color to the Summary worksheet tab.

7. With the Summary worksheet active, create a SUM formula with a 3-D reference in cell C6 that sums the hours for Lou Cortez for all four weeks.

8. Drag the fill handle from cell C6 to cell C14.

9. Make the Week1 worksheet active. In cell K6, type the formula =if(j6>40,j6-40,0), drag the fill handle from cell K6 to cell K14, and then calculate the total in cell K15. (This IF formula says that if the amount in cell J6 is greater than 40, subtract the amount in the cell from 40 and return the result. If the amount is less than 40, the formula will insert a zero in the cell.)

10. In cell L6, type the formula =(j6*b17)+(k6*b17*.5), drag the fill handle from cell L6 to cell L14 and then calculate the total in cell L15. If necessary, increase the width of column L to display all cell entries. (The formula multiplies the total number of hours by the pay rate in cell B17 and then adds that amount to the number of overtime hours multiplied by the pay rate in cell B17 multiplied by 0.5 since overtime pay is one-and-a-half times the pay rate.)

11. Copy and paste the formulas in columns K and L to complete the *Overtime Hours* and *Gross Pay* column entries in the Week2 through Week4 worksheets.

12. Make the Summary worksheet active and then enter the 3-D reference formulas in cell D6 and cell E6 to sum the overtime hours and gross pay for Lou Cortez from all four worksheets.

13. Copy the 3-D formulas in the range D6:E6 and paste to the range D7:E14.

14. Calculate the totals in the range C15:E15 and then apply the Accounting format to the cells in the *Gross Pay* column.

15. Group and print all five worksheets. ***Note: If you submit your work in hard copy, check with your instructor to see if you need to print two copies of the worksheets with one of the copies showing the cell formulas instead of the calculated results.***

16. Save and then close **4-WBPayroll.xlsx**.

Review 2   Formatting a Table; Sorting; Filtering; Inserting and Printing Comments

1. Open **WBJuneOrders.xlsx** and then save it with the name **4-WBJuneOrders**.

2. Select the range A3:E41 and then format it as a table using the Table Style Medium 4 table style (fourth column, first row in *Medium* section).

3. Make cell A42 active and then type the following text in the columns indicated. Press the Enter key after typing the amount.

   Item: Allspice
   Supplier: Chapman Wholesale Foods
   Unit: case
   Unit Price: 39.59
   Amount: 1

4. Make cell F3 active, type Total, and then press the Enter key.

5. With cell F4 active, type the formula =d4*e4 and then press the Enter key.

6. Click the Table Tools Design tab and then click the *Total Row* check box to insert a check mark.

7. Adjust the width of column F to display the entire amount in cell F43.

8. Filter the table to display only those items purchased from Chapman Wholesale Foods.

9. Print the filtered worksheet.
10. Redisplay all rows in the table.
11. Sort the table first by Supplier and then by Item with both levels in A to Z order.
12. Add a comment to cell C14 and type the text Dana, please check with JL Enterprises to determine if they sell carrots in 50 pound bags.
13. Add a comment to cell D18 and type the text Dana, I think we should negotiate with Sven to reduce this price.
14. Show all comments in the worksheet and set them to print as displayed on the worksheet.
15. Save and then print **4-WBJuneOrders.xlsx**.
16. Save the workbook in the PDF file format and specify that you want the file to open after publishing.
17. Print and then close the **4-WBJuneOrders.pdf** file.
18. Close **4-WBJuneOrders.xlsx**.

Review 3 Creating a Workbook Using a Template

1. Display the New backstage area, type billing statement in the search text box, and then press the Enter key. Download the billing statement template as shown in Figure WB-4.1.
2. Enter data into the template as shown in Figure WB-4.1.
3. Save the workbook with the name **4-PTStmntAug31**.

Figure WB-4.1 Review 3

The Waterfront Bistro

3104 Rivermist Drive
Buffalo, NY 14280

Phone: (716) 555-3166
Fax: (716) 555-3190
E-mail: accounts@wfbistro.emcp.net

Statement

Statement #:	101
Date:	Current Date
Customer ID:	PT-Sinclar

Bill To: Bobbie Sinclair
Performance Threads
4011 Bridgewater Street
Niagara Falls, ON L2E 2T6
CANADA

Date	Type	Invoice #	Description	Amount	Payment	Balance
8/10/2018	Dir Mtg	2462	Catering Services	$ 726.60		$ 726.60
					Total	$ 726.60

Reminder: Please include the statement number on your check.

Terms: Balance due in 30 days.

REMITTANCE	
Customer Name:	Enter customer name
Customer ID:	PT-Sinclar
Statement #:	101
Date:	Current Date
Amount Due:	$726.60
Amount Enclosed:	

4. Print and then close **4-PTStmntAug31.xlsx**.

Skills Assessment

NIAGARA PENINSULA COLLEGE

Data File

Assessment 1 Inserting, Deleting, and Renaming Worksheets; Linking Worksheets

1. Open **NPCInternGrades.xlsx** and then save it with the name **4-NPCInternGrades**.
2. Insert a new worksheet before the MarqueeProductions worksheet and rename the worksheet *GradeSummary*.
3. Delete Sheet3.
4. Finish the GradeSummary worksheet by completing the following tasks:
   a. Copy the range A3:B7 in MarqueeProductions to A3:B7 in GradeSummary, keeping the source column widths.
   b. Copy the range A4:B8 in PerformanceThreads to A8:B12 in GradeSummary.
   c. Copy the range G3:H3 in MarqueeProductions to C3:D3 in GradeSummary, keeping the source column widths.
   d. Link the cells in columns C and D of the GradeSummary worksheet to the corresponding grades and dates in MarqueeProductions and PerformanceThreads.
   e. Copy the title and subtitle in rows 1 and 2 from MarqueeProductions to GradeSummary.
   f. Change the font size of rows 1 and 2 in GradeSummary to 12 points and then merge and center columns A–D.
   g. Select the range E1:H2, click the Clear button in the Editing group, and then click the *Clear All* option at the drop-down list.
5. Change the left margin for the GradeSummary worksheet only to 3 inches.
6. Group the three worksheets and then change the page layout to landscape orientation.
7. Save, print all three worksheets, and then close **4-NPCInternGrades.xlsx**.

Performance Threads ## Assessment 2 Formatting a Table; Filtering; Sorting; Saving a Workbook in a Different Format

Data File

1. Open **PTMarqueeSch.xlsx** and then save it with the name **4-PTMarqueeSch**.
2. Select the range A5:H12 and then format it as a table using the Table Style Medium 25 table style (fourth column, fourth row in the *Medium* section).
3. Filter the table to show only those costumes with a final delivery date of 8/13/2018. *Note: Since **Start Date** and **End Date** are repeated as column headings in the table, Excel adds numbers after the first occurrences to make each column heading unique.*
4. Sort the filtered list by costume from A to Z.
5. Change to landscape orientation and then print the filtered and sorted list.
6. Redisplay all rows in the table.
7. Sort the table first by the final delivery date from oldest to newest and then by costume from A to Z.
8. Save and then print **4-PTMarqueeSch.xlsx**.
9. You need to send the workbook to a colleague using Open Office. Save the workbook in the OpenDocument Spreadsheet (*.ods) format with the same name.
10. Close **4-PTMarqueeSch.ods**.

Assessment 3 — Inserting and Printing Comments

1. Open **PTMarqueeSch.xlsx** and then save it with the name **4-PTMarqueeSchComments**.
2. Make cell D6 active and then add the comment Sue has not completed the research. Design may not be able to start June 10.
3. Make cell G9 active and then type These dates may need adjustment due to overlapping projects.
4. Show all comments.
5. Turn on printing of comments as displayed on the worksheet.
6. Save, print, and then close **4-PTMarqueeSchComments.xlsx**.

Assessment 4 — Formatting Columns and Formatting a Table; Saving a Workbook in PDF File Format

1. Open **PTRentalCost.xlsx** and then save it with the name **4-PTRentalCost**.
2. Select the range A3:F43 and then format it as a table using the Table Style Light 11 table style (fourth column, second row in the *Light* section).
3. Type Total Due in cell G3 and then press the Enter key.
4. With cell G4 active, type the formula =f4*c4.
5. Insert a total row at the bottom of the table.
6. Display the worksheet in Page Break Preview, adjust the page break so all data fits on one page, and then return the view to Normal.
7. Save and then print **4-PTRentalCost.xlsx**.
8. Save the workbook in the PDF file format and indicate that you want the file to open when published.
9. Print and then close the **4-PTRentalCost.pdf** file.
10. Close **4-PTRentalCost.xlsx**.

Assessment 5 — Finding Information on File Formats Not Supported by Excel 2016

1. Use Excel Help to search for information on file formats not supported in Excel 2016. (Search for the article File formats supported in Excel for Windows and then navigate below all of the file formats supported by Excel to view the file formats not supported by Excel.)
2. Create a table in a new worksheet that provides the file format, the extension, and any other identifying information. *Note: Copying and pasting information from the Excel Help window or a Microsoft website is not acceptable.*
3. Apply a table style to the table.
4. Make sure the information is easy to read and understand.
5. Make sure the table will fit on one page when printed.
6. Save the workbook with the name **4-FileFormats**.
7. Print and then close **4-FileFormats.xlsx**.

Assessment 6 Smartphone Shopping

1. After graduation, your goal is to work independently as a consultant in your field of study. You plan to travel frequently in North America and Europe. You want to purchase a smartphone to use while traveling for conference calling, emailing, web browsing, text messaging, and modifying Office documents. Research the latest product offerings for smartphones on the Internet.

2. Select three phones from three different manufacturers for your short-list comparison. Create a worksheet for analyzing the three smartphones, organizing the information in a table so that the main features are categorized in the leftmost column with each phone's specification for that feature next to each category. Make sure each smartphone's name or manufacturer is identified at the top of the respective columns. In the last row of the table, insert the estimated cost for each smartphone.

3. Based on your perception of the best value, select one of the phones as your recommendation and insert a comment in the phone's cost cell indicating your choice.

4. Add an image or other enhancements to improve the worksheet's appearance.

5. Save the workbook with the name **4-Smartphones**.

6. Print the worksheet in landscape orientation scaled to fit on one page and with the comment cell printed as displayed on the worksheet.

7. Save and then close **4-Smartphones.xlsx**.

Marquee Challenge

The Waterfront BISTRO

Challenge 1 Creating a Sales Invoice by Downloading a Template

1. Dana Hirsch has asked you to find and download a professionally designed sales invoice template and then use the template to create an invoice to be sent to First Choice Travel for catering their business meeting.

Data File

2. Open the New backstage area, type sales invoice blue gradient design in the search text box and then press Enter. Download the template named *Sales invoice (Blue Gradient design)* to your computer. If you cannot find the template shown in Figure WB-4.2, download another suitable template for a sales invoice.

3. Complete the customer invoice using the information found in Figure WB-4.2.

4. To insert the logo, select the logo container object, click the Insert tab, and then click the Pictures button in the Illustrations group. At the Insert Picture dialog box, navigate to the folder containing the **TWBLogo.jpg** file and then double-click **TWBLogo.jpg**. Move and resize the logo image as shown in Figure WB-4.2.

5. Delete the unused rows between the billing address and the body of the invoice.

6. Delete the unused rows between the last line item and the subtotal row.

7. Format the *QTY* column as shown in Figure WB-4.2.

8. Type The Waterfront Bistro next to *Make all checks payable to* near the bottom of the invoice.

9. Save the invoice with the name **4-WBInvFCT**.

10. Print and then close **4-WBInvFCT.xlsx**.

The Waterfront Bistro

INVOICE

3104 Rivermist Drive
Buffalo, NY 14280
(716) 555-3166
wfbistro@emcp.net

INVOICE NO.	2463
DATE	August 31, 2018
CUSTOMER ID	FCT-Torres

TO   Alex Torres
First Choice Travel
4277 Yonge Street
Toronto, ON M4P 2E6
(416) 555-9834

SHIP TO   2100 Victoria Street
Niagara on the Lake, ON L0S 1J0

QTY	ITEM #	DESCRIPTION	UNIT PRICE	DISCOUNT	LINE TOTAL
16.00		Lunches	$ 18.23		$ 291.68
16.00		Desserts	5.31		84.96
16.00		Beverages	1.87		29.92
1.00		Delivery and setup	65.00		65.00
			TOTAL DISCOUNT		
				SUBTOTAL	$ 471.56
				SALES TAX	9%
				TOTAL	$ 514.00

Worldwide Enterprises   Challenge 2   Importing, Formatting and Sorting a Distributor List

Data Files

1. Sam Vestering, manager of North American Distribution at Worldwide Enterprises, has provided you with two text files exported from the corporate head office computer. One file contains a list of US distributors and the other contains a list of Canadian distributors. Sam would like a one-page list of all distributors.

2. In Excel, display the Open dialog box with the folder containing the **WEUSDistributors.txt** file the active folder and then change the file type option (located to the right of the *File name* text box) to *All Files (*.*)*. Double-click **WEUSDistributors.txt** and then follow the steps in the Text Import Wizard. You only need to make a change in Step 2 of the wizard, and that is to change the delimiter to a comma.

3. Open the file named **WECdnDistributors.txt** and follow the steps in the Text Import Wizard.

4. Move or copy the data from one of the worksheets to the bottom of the other worksheet.

5. Widen columns as necessary and then delete the second address and email address columns.

6. Add the logo, title, and column labels above the data as shown in Figure WB-4.3. Use the Pictures button in the Illustrations group on the Insert tab to insert the logo file named **WELogo.jpg**.

7. Format the data as a table. Use your best judgment to determine the table style, column widths, and other formatting options to apply to the table as shown in Figure WB-4.3.
8. Look closely at Figure WB-4.3 to determine the sort order and then custom sort the table. *Hint: The table is sorted by three levels*.
9. Save the worksheet as an Excel file in the Workbook (*xlsx) file format and name it **4-WEDistributors**.
10. Apply the landscape orientation.
11. Display the worksheet in Page Break Preview, adjust the page break to ensure that the data fits on one page, and then return to Normal view.
12. Save, print, and then close **4-WEDistributors.xlsx**.
13. Close all other open workbooks without saving changes.

Figure WB-4.3 Challenge 2

Worldwide Enterprises	North American Distributor List					
Name	**Mailing Address**	**City**	**State**	**Zip Code**	**Telephone**	**Fax**
Olympic Cinemas	P.O. Box 1439	Calgary	AB	T2C 3P7	403-555-4587	403-555-4589
LaVista Cinemas	111 Vista Road	Phoenix	AZ	86355-6014	602-555-6231	602-555-6233
West Coast Movies	P.O. Box 298	Vancouver	BC	V6Y 1N9	604-555-3548	604-555-3549
Marquee Movies	1011 South Alameda Street	Los Angeles	CA	90045	612-555-2398	612-555-2377
Sunfest Cinemas	341 South Fourth Avenue	Tampa	FL	33562	813-555-3185	813-555-3177
Liberty Cinemas	P.O. Box 998	Atlanta	GA	73125	404-555-8113	404-555-2349
O'Shea Movies	59 Erie	Oak Park	IL	60302	312-555-7719	312-555-7381
Midtown Moviehouse	1033 Commercial Street	Emporia	KS	66801	316-555-7013	316-555-7022
All Nite Cinemas	2188 3rd Street	Louisville	KY	40201	502-555-4238	502-555-4240
Eastown Movie House	P.O. Box 722	Cambridge	MA	2142	413-555-0981	413-555-0226
Riverview Cinemas	1011-848 Sheppard Street	Winnipeg	MB	R2P 0N6	204-555-6538	204-555-6533
New Age Movies	73 Killarney Road	Moncton	NB	E1B 2Z9	506-555-8376	506-555-8377
EastCoast Cinemas	62 Mountbatten Drive	St.John's	NF	A1A 3X9	709-555-8349	709-555-8366
Hillman Cinemas	55 Kemble Avenue	Baking Ridge	NJ	7920	201-555-1147	201-555-1143
Seaboard Movie House Inc.	P.O. Box 1005	Dartmouth	NS	B2V 1Y8	902-555-3948	902-555-3950
Northern Reach Movies	P.O. Box 34	Yellowknife	NW	X1A 2N9	867-555-6314	867-555-6316
Mainstream Movies	P.O. Box 33	Buffalo	NY	14601	212-555-3269	212-555-3270
Victory Cinemas	12119 South 23rd	Buffalo	NY	14288	212-555-8746	212-555-8748
Waterfront Cinemas	P.O. Box 3255	New York	NY	14288	212-555-3845	212-555-3947
Westview Movies	1112 Broadway	New York	NY	10119	212-555-4875	212-555-4877
Mooretown Movies	P.O. Box 11	Dublin	OH	43107	614-555-8134	614-555-8339
Millennium Movies	4126 Yonge Street	Toronto	ON	M2P 2B8	416-555-9335	416-555-9338
Redwood Cinemas	P.O. Box 112F	Portland	OR	97466-3359	503-555-8641	503-555-8633
Wellington 10	1203 Tenth Southwest	Philadelphia	PA	19178	215-555-9045	215-555-9048
Waterdown Cinemas	575 Notre Dame Street	Summerside	PE	C1N 1T8	902-555-8374	902-555-8376
MountainView Movies	5417 RoyalMount Avenue	Montreal	PQ	H4P 1H8	514-555-3584	514-555-3585
Danforth Cinemas	P.O. Box 22	Columbia	SC	29201	803-555-3487	803-555-3421
Plains Cinema House	P.O. Box 209	Regina	SK	S4S 5Y9	306-555-1247	305-555-1248
Century Cinemas	3687 Avenue K	Arlington	TX	76013	817-555-2116	817-555-2119
Countryside Cinemas	22 Hillside Street	Bennington	VT	5201	802-555-1469	802-555-1470
Northern Stars Movies	811 Cook Street	Whitehorse	YK	Y1A 2S4	867-555-6598	867-555-6599

Study Tools

Study tools include a presentation and In Brief step lists. Use these resources to help you further develop and review skills learned in this section.

Recheck

SNAP Check your understanding by taking this quiz. If you are a SNAP user, launch the Recheck from your Assignments page.

Skills Review

Review 1   Copying and Pasting Data

1. With Word active, open **NPCWordScores.docx**.
2. Make Excel active and then open **NPCExcelScores.xlsx**.
3. Save the workbook with the name **1-NPCExcelScores**.
4. Click the Word button on the taskbar.
5. Select the nine lines of text in columns (the line beginning *Student* through the line beginning *Yiu, Terry*) and then click the Copy button in the Clipboard group on the Home tab.
6. Click the Excel button on the taskbar.
7. With cell A5 active, paste the text into the worksheet.
8. Select the range A5:A13, click the Delete button arrow in the Cells group on the Home tab, click *Delete Cells*, and then click OK at the Delete dialog box.
9. Increase the width of column A by double-clicking the gray column boundary line between columns A and B.
10. Select the range B6:D13 and then click once on the Increase Decimal button in the Number group on the Home tab. (This displays two decimal places after the decimal point.)
11. Type the word Average in cell E5.
12. Make cell E6 active. Insert a formula that averages the numbers in cells B6 through D6.
13. Using the fill handle, copy the formula in cell E6 to the range E7:E13.
14. With cells E6 through E13 selected, change the font to 12-point Cambria.
15. Select cells B6 through E13, click the Center button in the Alignment group on the Home tab, and then deselect the cells.
16. Save, print, and then close **1-NPCExcelScores.xlsx**.
17. Click the Word button on the taskbar and then close **NPCWordScores.docx**.

Review 2   Linking an Object and Editing a Linked Object

1. With Word active, open **NPCWordEnroll.docx**.
2. Save the document with the name **1-NPCWordEnroll**.
3. Make Excel active and then open **NPCExcelChart.xlsx**.
4. Save the workbook with the name **1-NPCExcelChart**.
5. Link the chart to the Word document a triple space below the *Student Enrollment* subtitle. (Make sure you use the Paste Special dialog box.)
6. Select the chart and then center it by clicking the Center button in the Paragraph group on the Home tab.
7. Save, print, and then close **1-NPCWordEnroll.docx**.
8. Click the Excel button on the taskbar.
9. Click outside the chart to deselect it.
10. Print **1-NPCExcelChart.xlsx** in landscape orientation.
11. With **1-NPCExcelChart.xlsx** open, make the following changes to the data in the specified cells:
    - A2: Change *Fall Term* to *Spring Term*.
    - B4: Change *75* to *98*.
    - B5: Change *30* to *25*.
    - B6: Change *15* to *23*.
    - B7: Change *38* to *52*.
    - B8: Change *25* to *10*.
12. Make cell A2 active.
13. Save, print in landscape orientation, and then close **1-NPCExcelChart.xlsx**.
14. Make Word active and then open **1-NPCWordEnroll.docx**. (At the message asking if you want to update the document, click Yes.)
15. Save, print, and then close **1-NPCWordEnroll.docx**.

Review 3   Embedding an Object

1. With Word active, open **WERevMemo.docx**.
2. Save the document with the name **1-WERevMemo**.
3. Make Excel active and then open **WEExcelRev.xlsx**.
4. Embed the data in the range A2:D8 in the Word document a double space below the paragraph of text in the body of the memo.
5. Save and then print **1-WERevMemo.docx**.
6. Click the Excel button on the taskbar, close **WEExcelRev.xlsx** without saving it, and then close Excel.
7. With **1-WERevMemo.docx** open, double-click the worksheet and then make the following changes to the data in the specified cells:
    - A2: Change *July Revenues* to *August Revenues*.
    - B4: Change *1,356,000* to *1,575,000*.
    - B5: Change *2,450,000* to *2,375,000*.
    - B6: Change *1,635,000* to *1,750,000*.
    - B7: Change *950,000* to *1,100,000*.
    - B8: Change *1,050,000* to *1,255,000*.
8. Click in cell A2 and then click outside the worksheet to deselect it.
9. In the memo document, change the date from *August 14, 2018* to *September 4, 2018* and change the subject from *July Revenues* to *August Revenues*.
10. Save, print, close **1-WERevMemo.docx**, and then close Word.